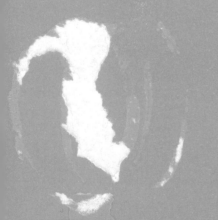

On the Front Line

SURVIVING THE HOLOCAUST

Cath Senker

www.raintreepublishers.co.uk
Visit our website to find out more information about **Raintree** books.

To order:
☎ Phone 44 (0) 1865 888113
▤ Send a fax to 44 (0) 1865 314091
💻 Visit the Raintree Bookshop at **www.raintreepublishers.co.uk** to browse our catalogue and order online.

Produced for Raintree by
White-Thomson Publishing Ltd,
Bridgewater Business Centre,
210 High Street, Lewes, BN7 2NH

First published in Great Britain by Raintree,
Halley Court, Jordan Hill, Oxford OX2 8EJ,
part of Harcourt Education.
Raintree is a registered trademark of
Harcourt Education Ltd.

Editorial: Juliet Smith and Daniel Nunn
Design: Michelle Lisseter
Picture Research: Elaine Fuoco-Lang
Project Manager: Juliet Smith
Production: Duncan Gilbert

Originated by Dot Gradations Ltd
Printed and bound in China by South China
Printing Company Ltd

ISBN 1 844 43694 2
09 08 07 06 05
10 9 8 7 6 5 4 3 2 1

British Library Cataloguing in Publication Data
Senker, Cath
Surviving the Holocaust. – (On the Front Line)
1. Holocaust, Jewish (1939–1945) – Juvenile literature
1. Title 940.5'318
A full catalogue record for this book is available from the British Library.

Acknowledgements
The publishers would like to thank the following for permission to reproduce photographs and maps: AKG images pp. **4-5**, **6** (l), **6-7**, **7** (r), **12** (l), **12** (r), **15**, **16**, **18**, **19**, **20**, **23**, **24**, **25**, **26-27**, **29**, **30**, **31**, **32-33**, **35**, **36**, **41**; Corbis p. **39**; Holocaust Memorial Museum Library pp. **5** (l), **9**, **10**, **14**; Michael Shocket p. **14** (l); Popperfoto pp. **17**, **37**; Topfoto pp. **8**, **11**, **19** (r), **21**, **22**, **24** (l), **27** (r), **28**, **28** (l), **32** (l), **34**, **38**, **40** (l); Zvi Kadushin/Beth Hatefutsoth, Nahum Goldmann Museum of Jewish Diaspora p. **18** (l). Cover photograph of prisoners freed from Oswiecim in January 1945, reproduced with permission of Topfoto. Map on p.13 by Jillian Luff.

The publishers would like to thank the following for permission to reproduce extracts: pp. **10–11** Story adapted from *The Necklace* by Lee Edwards, in *I Came Alone* edited by Bertha Leverton and Shmuel Lowensohn; letter adapted from a letter from the British Interaid Committee, 7 December 1938, from *I Came Alone*, p. 403; pp. **14–15** Anne Frank quote adapted from *Anne Frank: The Diary of a Young Girl* (Puffin, 1997).

Source notes: pp. **8–9** *Never Again* by Martin Gilbert, p. 43; pp. **10–11** *I Came Alone* edited by Bertha Leverton and Shmuel Lowensohn, p. 403; pp. **14–15** *Know Me Tomorrow* by Michael Shocket; pp. **16–17** *Never Again*, p. 55; Oswald Pohl quotation adapted from *The Camp System* by Pat Levy, p. 15; pp. **20–21** statistics from *Never Again* p. 71; pp. **22–23** Victor Breitburg's story from Lodz ShtetLinks http://www.shtetlinks.jewishgen.org/lodz/holocaust.htm#Testimonies; pp. **24–25** Poldek Pfefferberg quote from http://www.shoah.dk/Schindler/page_11.htm; pp. **26–27** Max Perkal from *Outside was Beautiful* by Max Perkal; pp. **30–31** Mendel Fiszlewicz from *Survival and Resistance* by Pat Levy, p. 39; pp. **32–33** from Yad Vashem, Israel; Abba Kovner quote from *Tough Jews* by Rich Cohen; pp. **34–35** Himmler quote from Jewish Virtual Library; pp. **36–37** death figures from *Introducing the Holocaust* by Haim Bresheeth, Stuart Hood, and Litza Jansz; pp. **38–39** Bella's story from the Nizkor Project.

Every effort has been made to contact copyright holders of any material reproduced in this book. Any omissions will be rectified in subsequent printings if notice is given to the publishers.

The paper used to print this book comes from sustainable resources.

CONTENTS

Any words appearing in the text in bold, **like this**, are explained in the glossary. You can also look out for them in the Word Bank box at the bottom of each page.

Leon Greenman was born in London in 1910. Leon was Jewish. Leon, his wife, and little boy were in Rotterdam, in **the Netherlands**, when World War II began in September 1939. In May 1940, Germany invaded the Netherlands. The German leaders, called **Nazis**, passed laws that made life almost impossible for Jewish people.

Trapped

Leon knew that he and his family were in terrible danger. He was trapped in a country that had been taken over by the Nazis – who were not only at war with England, but also hated Jewish people. Leon had to think quickly.

What was the Holocaust?

Between 1933 and 1945, the National Socialist (Nazi) Party was in power in Germany. In 1942, the Nazis brought in a policy called the "Final Solution". Its aim was to kill all the Jews in Europe. By the time the Nazis were defeated in 1945 they had murdered about 6 million Jews. The Nazis also murdered **Roma** (gypsies), gay people, disabled people, and people with different political views. These killings are known as the Holocaust.

In January 1945, the Soviet army freed these prisoners from the Auschwitz camp in Poland.

Word Bank death **camp** camp where the Nazis sent Jews and others to be killed
Holocaust the killing of millions of Jews and others by the Nazis

He left his passport with Dutch friends to look after, but they burned it. They were frightened the Nazis would catch them with it.

In October 1942, the Nazis went hunting for Jews. They loaded Leon and his family on to a railway train to the Auschwitz-Birkenau death camp. At Auschwitz, the men were ordered to one side of the camp, and women and children to the other. Leon never saw his wife and son again.

Survival

In Auschwitz, Leon was tough enough to survive three years of terrible hard work in several labour camps. Leon was one of very few who survived Auschwitz and lived to tell the tale. He now travels around talking about the Holocaust.

Find out later

How did some Jewish people hide from the Nazis?

Which countries helped Jews to escape?

What happened to people who survived the Holocaust?

Nazis people in the political party that ran Germany from 1933 to 1945
the Netherlands country in Western Europe, also called Holland

THE NAZIS AND THE HOLOCAUST

This Nazi poster encouraged people to help the homeless. It says "Build Youth Hostels and Homes".

In 1918, Germany lost World War I. Because it lost the war, it had to pay a lot of money to the countries that won the war. It had to give away much of its richest land. All of this made Germany very poor. German industries were not making much money and millions of people lost their jobs.

The Nazi Party

In 1919, a political party called the **Nazi** Party (National Socialist Party) was set up. Adolf Hitler became its leader in 1921. The Nazis thought that **Aryans** – white-skinned Europeans – were a "master race" and were better than all other people.

Unemployment figures

The Nazis grew more popular in Germany as the number of people without jobs increased:

1928 → 1.9 million
1929 → 2.9 million
1930 → 3.2 million
1931 → 4.9 million
1932 → 6 million

Word Bank   Aryans   people from Germany and Scandinavia whom the Nazis thought were superior to everyone else

The Nazis blamed other people, especially the Jews, for Germany's problems. In the late 1920s, the Nazi Party tried to get people to vote them into the government. The Nazi Party also set up the "Stormtroopers" (often known as "Brownshirts"). The Brownshirts bullied people into voting for the Nazi Party.

Hitler's promise

In 1929, the **Great Depression** began in the United States, which could then no longer put money into German businesses. Germany's problems became worse. Hitler promised he would win back German land and give everyone jobs. Many people believed him and, in January 1933, he was asked to become leader of Germany.

> **Nazi views**
> The Nazis set out their views in 1920:
> "Only people of German blood can be members of our nation, whatever their religion.
> No Jewish person may be a member of the nation."

Here, hundreds of men queue outside a factory in Hanover, Germany, in 1930 in the hope of finding some work.

Adolf Hitler, the leader of the German Nazi Party.

Great Depression the time from 1929 to 1939 when the US and European economies were doing very badly. Many people were poor and without jobs.

Hitler in power

In March 1933, an Act of the German Parliament made Hitler a **dictator**. He could pass whatever laws he liked. The Nazi Party was the only political party allowed. The **Nazis** took over the **trade unions**. From May 1933, all workers had to belong to the Nazi trade union. At age 13, boys had to join the Hitler Youth Movement, and learn Nazi ideas. Girls joined the League of German Girls. Hitler set up work projects, such as road building, to give people jobs. He built factories to make weapons. Hitler planned to go to war to win back the land Germany had lost.

Rabbi Schonfeld

In the mid-1930s, Jews could only escape to the United Kingdom if British people would look after them, because the British Government did not want to pay for their care. Rabbi Schonfeld was working in England when he decided to arrange for **refugees** to live with Jewish families in the United Kingdom. He rescued over 3700 people and saved their lives.

These boys from the Hitler Youth Movement are marching in the street to show the strength of their organization.

Word Bank

dictator	ruler who has complete power over a country
refugees	people who are forced to leave their country

Jews forced out!

Jewish people were not allowed to mix with other Germans. They lost their jobs and had to sell their businesses. Many Jews left the country if they could. In November 1938, the Nazis destroyed thousands of Jewish shops and many **synagogues** in Germany and Austria. The event became known as *Kristallnacht* – The Night of Broken Glass.

Prisons

In 1939, the Nazis set up prisons called **concentration camps**. They sent Jews, gay people, **Roma** (also known as gypsies), and anyone who disagreed with them to the camps. The Nazis did not believe in spending money on disabled people. Between October 1939 and August 1941, they murdered more than 70,000 disabled people.

Terror and violence

German-Jewish teenager Eric Lucas described what happened in his village during *Kristallnacht*:

"Suddenly, the gathering outside the synagogue brought out axes and sledgehammers [heavy hammers]. They cried 'Down with the Jews'. They ran towards it and burst open the door. The crowd stormed in, shouting and laughing."

During *Kristallnacht*, the inside of this synagogue in Hechingen, south-west Germany, was completely destroyed.

synagogues Jewish places of worship

Operation *Kindertransports*

After *Kristallnacht*, the British Government allowed up to 10,000 mostly Jewish children from Germany, Austria, and Czechoslovakia to come to England. They had to come without their parents. This was known as "Operation Kindertransports" (meaning transport for children).
Lee Edwards was fifteen when she left Germany on a *Kindertransport* in 1939. Lee could see her mother crying when she said goodbye to her. They never met again.

Lee went by train to **the Netherlands** and then by boat to England. When she arrived, the **customs officers** opened Lee's suitcase. She noticed a pretty necklace from her mother in the suitcase.

These Jewish refugee children from the first *Kindertransport* from Germany have just arrived in Harwich, England.

Word Bank   **customs officers** workers who check people's bags when they arrive in a different country. They make sure people have not brought in illegal goods.

A new life

Lee went to live with a Jewish family in Coventry, England. There was often heavy bombing during World War II. During these frightening times, Lee held the necklace for comfort.

Sad news

After the war, Lee found out that her mother had died in Auschwitz-Birkenau **death camp**. Her father had killed himself. Lee's brother managed to survive many years in a **concentration camp**. Lee eventually went to work for the US army in Germany. She met her husband, another **refugee**, in 1947. They eventually settled in Los Angeles, California, in the United States. Lee still remembers her mother, who saved her life by sending her away. She will treasure the necklace for ever.

Jewish children in the Holocaust

This is what happened to Jewish children in the Holocaust:

- Nearly 30,000 children survived in hiding
- About 10,000 (mostly Jewish) came to the United Kingdom from Germany, Austria, and Czechoslovakia
- Around 1.5 million died.

A young Jewish-German refugee arrives in England with her dolls.

UNDER NAZI OCCUPATION

Who are the Roma?

The Roma (sometimes called gypsies or Romanies) are a travelling people with their own language and way of life. They used to work as animal traders and tinkers (people who went from place to place selling or mending things). The Nazis hated the Roma and tried to wipe them out.

In 1938, Hitler's armies occupied Austria and took over part of Czechoslovakia. The following March they occupied the rest of Czechoslovakia. In September 1939, they invaded Poland, and the United Kingdom and France declared war on Germany. In 1940, German armies invaded Denmark, Norway, Belgium, **the Netherlands**, and France and set up Nazi governments. Part of France kept its own government. The **Nazis** stopped Jews from mixing with non-Jews. They murdered many people opposed to Nazi rule.

Ghettos and labour camps

The Nazis forced all Jews to move to run-down parts of their towns. These areas became known as **ghettos**. They also set up slave **labour camps,** where Jews were worked to death.

It is 1939 and Hitler inspects his soldiers, who have just invaded Poland.

A group of Roma in Belzec labour camp, Poland, in 1942.

Word Bank   death squads groups of Nazis whose job it was to shoot Jews
deport   force someone to move to another country

The Nazis sent many non-Jews to ghettos and labour camps, too. For example, they forced the German **Roma** (gypsies) to live within Jewish ghettos in Poland. In June 1941, the German army invaded the **Soviet Union**. Now the Nazis controlled a vast area of Europe. They set up **death squads** to murder Jews in large numbers. In October 1941, they began to **deport** Jews from the countries under Nazi rule. They sent them to ghettos or to slave labour camps in Poland.

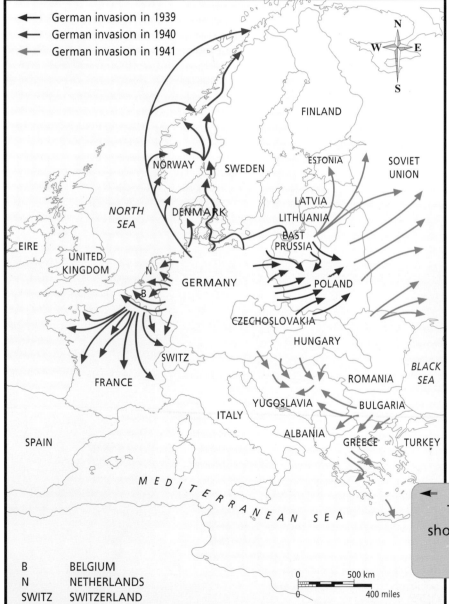

- German invasion in 1939
- German invasion in 1940
- German invasion in 1941

FINLAND

NORWAY SWEDEN ESTONIA SOVIET UNION

NORTH SEA DENMARK LATVIA LITHUANIA

EIRE UNITED KINGDOM EAST PRUSSIA

N GERMANY POLAND

B

CZECHOSLOVAKIA

SWITZ HUNGARY

FRANCE ROMANIA BLACK SEA

YUGOSLAVIA BULGARIA

ITALY ALBANIA

SPAIN GREECE TURKEY

M E D I T E R R A N E A N   S E A

B BELGIUM
N NETHERLANDS
SWITZ SWITZERLAND

0 ——— 500 km
0 ——— 400 miles

This is a map of Europe showing Germany's invasions up to 1941.

Nazi camps

There were three kinds of Nazi prisons:

- **Concentration camps** – the Nazis said these were for teaching their enemies to be Nazis, but in fact many died there.

- **Slave labour camps** – where prisoners were forced to work for the Nazis.

- **Death camps** – where Jews were sent to be killed.

Some camps were used for more than one purpose. For example, some people worked at death camps, and many people were killed in all three types of camp.

ghettos part of a town with a wall around it, where Jewish people had to live

Irène's story

Irène Rusak and her family lived in Brussels, Belgium. In 1940, when she was 13, the **Nazis** invaded Belgium. In 1942, the Nazis **deported** Eva, the eldest of Irène's sisters, to Auschwitz. She was gassed to death as soon as she reached the camp.

Shelter in a convent

Next, Irène's parents hid their second-oldest daughter, Ida, with a non-Jewish family. Her parents then travelled to many **convents** looking for shelter for Irène and her two other sisters. Finally, they found a convent that would take them in. The girls quickly learned all the Christian prayers so the other girls would not find out they were Jewish.

Irène in later life, after she married and went to live in England.

The hidden children

Some Jewish children survived because their parents gave them to kind non-Jewish people, such as the Belgian monk Father Bruno. They had to pretend to be Christians. A few Jewish children survived all alone, hiding in forests and barns.

Father Bruno poses with five Jewish children he is sheltering.

Word Bank   annexe   building added on to another building to give more space

Anne Frank in hiding

Anne Frank and her family were German Jews. When Hitler came to power in 1933, they fled to **the Netherlands**. In 1940, the Nazis invaded the Netherlands. Two years later, they started to deport Jews to the camps. Anne was now 13.

The secret annexe

Anne's family hid in a secret **annexe** above her father's office. Another Jewish family joined them. They had to remain hidden and stay quiet at all times. Some of the office workers would bring food and other things to them. Two years later, the Nazis discovered the families and deported them to Auschwitz camp. Only Anne's father, Otto, survived the camp and the **Holocaust**.

"When I think about our lives here, I usually think that we live in a paradise compared to the Jews who aren't in hiding."

An extract from Anne Frank's diary.

Anne Frank (third from right) walks next to her father, Otto, in happier days.

convent   place where nuns live and work

Arek Hersh

Arek Hersh was 11 when he was sent to Otoczno slave **labour camp** in Poland. Prisoners in slave labour camps had to work for 14 hours a day. Many workers tried to kill themselves by jumping under trains. The **Nazis** murdered prisoners for breaking the rules. Arek remembered one guard called Rudi. He killed prisoners by **hacking** them to death with a spade.

Dying of hunger

The prisoners in Otoczno were always starving hungry. Each day they were given only one small piece of bread, some black coffee, a little watery soup, and nothing else! Some prisoners died of hunger. Life became tougher as time went on.

Polish men, and boys like Arek, were sent to work in labour camps.

Word Bank hacking cut with rough, heavy blows

There was less food and the prisoners had to work harder and harder. There was only one Nazi doctor for the whole camp. He did not have any medicines.

The camp started with 2500 men. Eighteen months later, only 11 were still alive; Arek was one of them. He was sent to several other camps and finally to Auschwitz. His strong will kept him going.

After the war

Arek survived the war and went to England. No one else in his family was still alive. All 80 of his family had died in the **Holocaust**.

Worked to death

In April 1942, Nazi Oswald Pohl organized war work in the camps. He ordered:

"Camp commanders must make sure people work as hard as they can. There are no limits to working hours. Keep mealtimes as short as possible."

This photo, taken in February 1941, shows prisoners making clothes in the **concentration camp** in Sachsenhausen.

LIFE IN THE GHETTOS

Secret photos

The Nazis took some photos themselves. They did not allow Jewish people to take photos. Some, such as the Jewish photographer Zvi Kadushin in the Kovno ghetto in Poland, took photos secretly. Zvi took most of his outdoor photos through a buttonhole in his coat. He took the photo below in 1941.

The **Nazis** had set up Jewish **ghettos** in poor parts of towns in 1939. They wanted to separate Jews from non-Jews. Jewish people had to move to the ghettos. The Nazis built walls around the ghettos. Armed guards stood at the gates to make sure that Jews did not escape.

In 1941, the Nazis decided to **deport** all the Jews from Germany, Austria, and Czechoslovakia to ghettos in Poland. They crammed huge numbers of people into the ghettos. Whole families had to live in one room. There was little work to do. The Nazis gave people **rations,** but there was never enough to eat. The Nazis chose people from the ghettos to form **Jewish Councils.** The Jewish Councils had to follow Nazi orders and run the ghettos. They gave out rations and organized Jewish police forces.

Word Bank   Jewish Councils   groups of Jewish people chosen to run a ghetto

Surviving the ghettos

Jewish people did their best to survive. They made things to sell outside the ghetto. Where there was soil, they grew vegetables. A few brave people sneaked out of the ghetto to buy food. People helped each other. They ran schools for the children. Performers put on concerts and plays to cheer people up, but life was extremely hard. Many people died of hunger and disease. There were Jewish doctors in the ghettos, but it was very hard to find medicine.

An underground (secret) school in the Lodz ghetto.

The Jewish Councils

People on the Jewish Councils had to do their job – or be killed. Some believed that if they did what the Nazis wanted, the Nazis might save some Jews. Others refused to follow Nazi orders. Whatever they did, most died.

The market in the Warsaw ghetto in Poland in 1941, where people came to exchange the few goods they had. Between July and December 1941, almost 30,000 Jews died of starvation in Warsaw.

rations small amounts of food and fuel given to people so they can survive

Victor Breitburg and the Lodz ghetto

Victor Breitburg survived the Lodz **ghetto** and Auschwitz. Victor lived in the Lodz ghetto from April 1941 to August 1944. In 1941 he was just 14 years old.

Victor lived in one small room with his sister, brother, and parents. People in the ghetto were starving. Many suffered from **tuberculosis**. Victor was lucky. He had a job in a woodworking factory, so he received extra food. He brought home sawdust from the factory and the family burned it to heat their small room.

Taken away

Everyone lived in fear of being sent away from the ghetto. In September 1942, the **Nazis** removed all the patients from the hospital. They also wanted to **deport** 25,000 Jews under 10 and over 65 years old from the ghetto. Victor and his father found a tunnel. They hid seventeen small children and their mothers from their building in the tunnel.

All Jewish people, such as this man in the Lodz ghetto in 1942, had to wear a yellow **Star of David**. The Nazis did not let anyone enter or leave the ghetto.

Word Bank   gas chambers   rooms used by the Nazis to gas people to death
Star of David   symbol of Jewish identity

Sole survivors

In June 1944, Victor's family was sent to Auschwitz-Birkenau. Victor's mother, sister, and brother were all killed in the **gas chambers**. Victor was selected to work at Auschwitz. He survived the war and went to New York in the United States. The rest of his family, except one cousin, had all been murdered.

Jewish photographer Mendel Grossman took photos secretly in the Lodz ghetto. Here, a boy feeds his little sister.

Life in the ghetto

Victor Breitburg remembers his life in the Lodz ghetto:

"I was sixteen and I'd never been out with a girl. I had a crush on a girl called Gisela, who lived in our building. Gisela and her parents were deported. Later, I found out she died in Chelmo gas chamber."

tuberculosis serious lung disease

The murder plan

In January 1942, the **Nazis** held a special meeting, known as the Wannsee Conference. They decided on a new policy to get rid of the Jews forever. This policy was called the "Final Solution". The Nazis wanted to empty the **ghettos** and **concentration camps**. They told the **Jewish Councils** in the ghettos to select groups of people to be **resettled** elsewhere. The Nazis did not explain what would happen to them. Some people **resisted**. For example, in October 1942, the Nazis **deported** 22,000 Jews from Piotrkow ghetto in Poland to Treblinka **death camp**. Two thousand Jews managed to hide. The Nazis hunted them down. They took those they caught to the forest, and shot them dead.

List of death

Adolf Eichmann was a Nazi leader. He made a list for the Wannsee Conference that showed the number of Jews the Nazis wanted to deport and kill:

- 4.5 million in countries under German rule
- 6.8 million in countries not under German rule
- More than 11 million in total.

These Dutch Jews in Westerbork camp, Holland, are being sent by train to Auschwitz in 1942.

Word Bank   Allies countries such as the United Kingdom, France, and the United States that fought against Nazi Germany

Off to the camps

All the Jews from the ghettos and concentration camps were sent to death or **labour camps** in Poland. The fittest went to labour camps. They had to work until they died from hunger, illness or exhaustion. The Nazis took everyone else to death camps. In these camps, the Jews were taken into **gas chambers** and murdered using poisonous gas.

Few survivors

A few workers with useful skills were allowed to stay in the ghettos. By 1944, however, the Nazis had closed all the ghettos. Almost everyone had been sent to death camps. Some had gone to labour camps. Only a few survived until the **Allies** freed them at the end of the war.

Heinrich Himmler (1900–1945)

Heinrich Himmler was a Nazi politician and military commander. He became the second most powerful man, after Hitler. In 1941, he took charge of the **death squads** that killed about half a million Jews in Eastern Europe. From December 1941, he organized the death camps in Poland.

Himmler (in the car) talks to a Jew living in the Lodz ghetto during his visit in 1942.

resettled moved to another place to live
resisted fought back and refused to do as they were told

23

STRUGGLING FOR SURVIVAL

From December 1941, many people were already dying in **concentration camps** and **labour camps**. The **Nazis**, however, wanted a more efficient way of killing the Jews. That year, they set up **death camps** in Poland to kill large numbers of people as quickly as possible. The death camps were Chelmo, Belzec, Sobibor, Treblinka, Madjanek, and Auschwitz. Madjanek and Auschwitz were also labour camps. The **SS**, Hitler's brutal bodyguards, ran the death camps.

Avoiding the camps

Oskar Schindler (seen above second left with some of the Jews he saved) was a German businessman. From 1943 to 1945, he ran a factory in Poland using Jewish workers. He **bribed** officials to save his workers from being sent to Auschwitz or other labour camps. Schindler saved about 1000 Jews from the gas chamber.

Gas chambers

At the death camps, there were **gas chambers**. When people arrived at a camp, they were sent straight to the gas chambers. The Nazis said the chambers were showers.

This gas chamber was used in the Auschwitz concentration camp.

Word Bank   bribed   gave something, such as money or favours, to someone in order to get them to behave in a certain way

When the victims went into them, poison gas came out, not water. They all choked to death. Then their bodies were burned in large ovens.

Terrible tasks

Just a few Jews were saved, to do horrible jobs. They formed the *Sonderkommando*, the "Special Commando" prisoner unit. These prisoners had to clean out the ovens and bury the ashes of the dead. They sorted the dead people's belongings, which were then sent for use in Germany. It is thought that at least 2 million Jews were killed in Chelmo, Belzec, Sobibor, and Treblinka between December 1941 and October 1943. About 52,000 **Roma** were also murdered.

> Prisoners were forced to do many horrible things. These prisoners are being treated like animals and are being forced to pull a trailer.

Schindler's children
Poldek Pffefferberg was saved by Oskar Schindler. He remembers:

"Schindler called us his children. In 1944 he was a wealthy man... he could have taken the money and gone to Switzerland... But instead he risked his life and all his money to save us."

SS   special police force, set up in 1925, as Hitler's personal guards. The SS later ran the death camps.

25

Max Perkal

Max Perkal was born in 1926 in Pruzany, Poland. Before the war, his father ran a small business. Max had a sister and two brothers. When the Germans came in 1941, the family had to move to a Jewish **ghetto**. In January 1943, when Max was 17, his family was sent to Auschwitz. The women and children were separated from the men. There was no time to say goodbye. Max was put to work. At first, he had to carry the belongings left by the people who had just been murdered. He saw people go to the **gas chambers** and he saw them after they had been killed by the gas.

Working for the enemy

In December 1943, Max was sent to work in the Auschwitz arms factory. He had to work solidly for 12 hours a day.

These Hungarian Jews are arriving in Auschwitz in 1944. Very soon after this photo was taken, most of these people were killed. ➤

His job was to make weapons. Somehow he survived more than a year of back-breaking labour.

Free at last

In January 1945, as the Soviet army moved closer to the camps in Poland, the **Nazis** emptied Auschwitz camp. Max ended up at Buchenwald **concentration camp**. Three months later, US soldiers freed the surviving prisoners. In June 1945, Max travelled to Switzerland, and later moved to the United States. He was the only member of his family to survive the **Holocaust**.

Kitty Hart

Kitty Hart was a Jewish girl from Poland. In 1942, her father bought fake **ID papers** for Kitty and her mother. The women had to take jobs as slave workers in a German factory. (About 5 million people from countries taken over by the **Nazis** were sent to work in Germany.) Kitty was only 14 years old. A year later, somebody told the Nazis that Kitty and her mother were Jews. They were sent to Auschwitz **labour camp**.

"You'll get out"

On her first night, a **Roma** woman read Kitty's palm. She said Kitty would leave Auschwitz alive. The following morning, the woman was dead.

This young woman has been forced to work in an arms factory in Germany.

Prisoners in the Belsen concentration camp became horribly thin.

How did some people survive?

Some prisoners survived because they were useful in running the camp. They included doctors, nurses, dentists, and musicians. These people were given extra **rations** and good clothes. Just a few survived after falling ill and gaining back some strength in hospital.

Word Bank   ID papers   Nazi identity papers that included the person's name and showed if he or she was Aryan, Jewish, or Roma

Basic essentials

Each prisoner had a bowl, which was both a food bowl and a toilet. There was nowhere to wash the bowl – or themselves. Kitty washed in her own urine to look clean. If prisoners looked dirty, they could be selected to die.

Horrible jobs

For eight months, Kitty worked in neighbouring Birkenau **death camp**. She sorted the belongings of the people who had been gassed. Another job was scooping up **excrement**. Kitty and her mother survived twenty months in Auschwitz. She was 17 when the Americans freed them. Her father had died in the camp and her brother had died fighting with the **partisans**.

Life in Auschwitz

Kitty Hart survived Auschwitz, but life was hard:

"I saw myself as a fox, avoiding the hunters. If you're afraid, you must creep away. You mustn't fight. That was my own way of surviving. It was best not to think. If you started to think, you were finished."

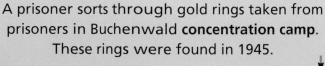

A prisoner sorts through gold rings taken from prisoners in Buchenwald **concentration camp**. These rings were found in 1945.

RESISTANCE!

A few countries refused **Nazi** orders to **deport** Jews to their deaths. In Finland in 1943, eight Jews were deported to Auschwitz. This caused big **protests**, however, and no one else was deported. The Nazis invaded Denmark in 1940. In 1943, they planned to deport the Jews, but Danish sailors shipped almost all of them to safety in Sweden.

Protests

No Jews were deported from Italy until the Nazis occupied the country in 1943. In the same year, the Nazis ordered its ally Bulgaria to deport its Jews. The Bulgarian people, including church leaders, organized huge protests. The protests stopped the government from deporting the Jews. In some European countries, brave people saved Jewish lives.

Punished for resistance

The Nazis killed resisters and punished their communities. In January 1943, Mendel Fiszlewicz attacked the German commander in Częstochowa, Poland. The Nazis quickly killed him. They then shot 25 men and sent 300 women and children to Treblinka death camp.

These Soviet partisans in 1943 are taking a break as they prepare for their next battle with the Nazis.

Word Bank protest occasion when people show that they disagree with, or do not approve of, something

In **the Netherlands**, Dutch people sheltered 20,000 Jews. Jews who lived in parts of France were smuggled into Spain. Spain stayed out of World War II.

Fighting and rebelling

In countries such as France, Poland, and the **Soviet Union**, people formed **partisan** groups to attack the Nazis. There were also Jewish partisan groups. As well as fighting, they sheltered Jews who had escaped from the Nazis. There were **rebellions** against the Nazis in the **ghettos**. The most famous was the Warsaw ghetto uprising in 1943 in Poland. There were even brave acts of **resistance** in the **death camps** and slave **labour camps**.

Fighting back

The Commander of **SS** forces near Sobibor death camp reported a rebellion in October 1943. He said:

"At about 5 p.m.; Jews attacked the guards and grabbed their guns. They killed 12 guards, and about 300 Jews escaped. The rest were shot to death, or have been brought back."

These German soldiers are taking photographs of a Soviet partisan who has been killed by the Nazis in 1942.

rebellion   when a group of people join together to fight against the people who are in power

Vitka Kempner

Vitka Kempner grew up in Kalish, a town near Vilna in Poland. The Germans invaded Kalish on the second day of the war. They sent the Jews away to a **monastery**. Nineteen-year-old Vitka escaped, along with other young Jews. In June 1941, the **Nazis** occupied Vilna. They began to round up the men. At the time, Jewish people did not know where their people were being taken to. They did not understand why they never came back.

A daring plan

In 1942, some Jews in Vilna formed an **underground movement** to fight the Nazis. The following year, Vitka's group of **partisans** carried out a daring and dangerous mission.

Partisan movements

Between 20,000 and 30,000 Jews escaped from the ghettos and **labour camps** and formed Jewish partisan movements. They destroyed thousands of German trains, and many power plants and factories. The partisans around Vilna in Poland killed more than 3000 German soldiers.

Soviet partisans made sure their weapons were clean and ready for action.

Word Bank monastery place where monks live and work

To plan it, Vitka had to go in and out of the **ghetto**. If the Nazi guards had caught her, they would have killed her on the spot. Vitka's group blew up the railway and damaged a German train carrying military equipment. There were great celebrations in the ghetto afterwards.

The end of the ghetto

In September 1943, the Nazis destroyed the Vilna ghetto. The fighters fled through the sewers. Vitka joined a Jewish partisan group, living rough in the forest. They fought the Nazis by bombing Vilna, destroying the water works and the power plant. Vitka survived the **Holocaust**. She married underground leader Abba Kovner and they moved to **Palestine** in 1946.

> ### A terrible choice
> Abba Kovner described the choice that Jewish people faced:
> "If we are cowards, we die. If we are brave, we die. So we might as well act bravely."

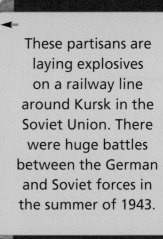

These partisans are laying explosives on a railway line around Kursk in the Soviet Union. There were huge battles between the German and Soviet forces in the summer of 1943.

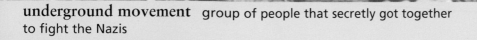

underground movement group of people that secretly got together to fight the Nazis

Marek Edelman

Marek Edelman was born to a Jewish family in 1921. He was brought up in Warsaw, Poland. His parents both died when he was a child. The **Nazis** occupied Warsaw in 1939. In 1940, they forced all the Jews into the Warsaw **ghetto**.

The Jewish Fighting Organization

Between July and September 1942, the Nazis sent about 300,000 Jews to Treblinka **death camp**. Marek and other young Jewish people set up the Jewish Fighting Organization to **resist** the Nazis. In January 1943, Jewish fighters fired on Nazis who came to **deport** more Jews. The Fighting Organization prepared for battle. The Polish **underground movement smuggled** guns into the ghetto to help the Jewish fighters.

Call for action

A call from the Jewish Fighting Organization, autumn 1942:

"Jewish people, the time has come. You must be prepared to resist. Not a single Jew should go to the railroad cars. If you can't fight, go into hiding."

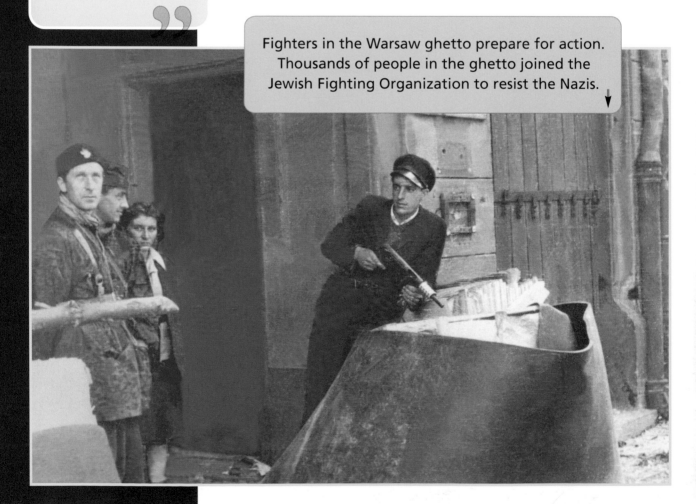

Fighters in the Warsaw ghetto prepare for action. Thousands of people in the ghetto joined the Jewish Fighting Organization to resist the Nazis.

Word Bank   command post   underground shelter for fighters in the ghettos

Battle for the ghetto

On 19 April 1943, the Nazis entered the ghetto again. The Fighting Organization fired on them. Marek Edelman led one of the four battle groups.

The **SS** began to burn down all the buildings in the ghetto. They rounded up all those who escaped the flames. On 8 May they attacked the fighters' **command post**. Marek was one of the few who managed to escape through the sewers. By 16 May the Germans had destroyed the whole ghetto. Seven thousand Jews had died and 50,000 were deported to **death camps** and **concentration camps**. Marek joined the Polish underground movement and he survived the war.

A group of SS men in the Warsaw ghetto during the uprising in 1943. They burned down the buildings to stop the resistance.

Fire everywhere

Mark Edelman remembers the terrible day the Nazis set fire to the Warsaw ghetto:

"The flames did what the Germans could not do. The smell of burning bodies was everywhere. The flames chased the people out of their shelters. The Germans caught them or shot them dead on the spot."

smuggle   move goods or people secretly

AFTER THE HORROR

Deaths in the Holocaust

Millions of men, women and children died during the Holocaust:

- about 6 million Jews

- over 3 million other Soviet prisoners of war

- 2 million other Soviet **civilians**

- over 1 million other Polish civilians

- over 1 million other Yugoslav civilians

- at least 200,000 disabled and elderly people

- over 200,000 **Roma**.

World War II ends

From June 1944, the **Nazis** started to lose the war. In January 1945, Soviet soldiers reached Auschwitz. They freed the few prisoners who were still alive. In April, British and US troops freed the survivors in Buchenwald, Belsen, and Dachau camps. In May, the war in Europe finally ended. The **Allies** had received reports about the **death camps** since December 1941. They were not sure whether to believe them. The troops who first saw the camp survivors were shocked. They were horribly thin – little more than skeletons. Hundreds of dead bodies lay everywhere.

US soldiers in Buchenwald **concentration camp**, just after they freed it in April 1945. They came too late for the dead prisoners in this trailer.

Word Bank　　civilian　person who is not in the army

The survivors

About two-thirds of the Jews of Europe had died in the **Holocaust**. The people who had been most likely to survive were rich people. They could afford to escape to other countries. A small number of prisoners who were very strong or lucky survived. They were very few compared to the number that died. Many survivors felt ashamed about surviving. Some killed themselves. After the war, Jewish survivors went back to their home countries or moved abroad. About 40,000 went to the United States, and around 83,000 moved to **Palestine**. In 1948, the Jewish State of Israel was formed there.

The Nuremberg Trials

In 1945–1946 some of the leading Nazis were put on trial in Nuremberg, Germany. The trials found over nineteen important leaders guilty of war crimes. Twelve were put to death, but many Nazis escaped trial. Shown below are Hermann Goering (A), commander-in-chief of the German air force, and Rudolph Hess (B), Hitler's deputy (second in command).

Bella Azar

Bella Azar was born in Iasi, Romania, in 1932. She had a brother and a sister. Her father was sent away to a slave **labour camp** in 1940. He never returned. In 1941, thousands of Jews in Iasi were robbed, beaten, and killed. A German officer beat up nine-year-old Bella in the street.

In the orphanage

In 1942, Bella's mother placed Bella and her sister Esther in an **orphanage** for safety. They stayed there until 1945. The children had to work hard, but they survived the **Holocaust**. After the war, a **Zionist** organization helped Bella and other Jewish orphans to move to **Palestine**.

The parents of these Jewish children all died in **concentration camps**. The children are being sent to live with the Jewish community in Palestine. ➔

Word Bank   kibbutz (plural **kibbutzim**)   community set up by some Jewish people who settled in Palestine

Moving to Israel

In 1947, a Zionist organization gathered about 500 children and took them to **the Netherlands**. They learnt Hebrew, Jewish history, and maths. The following year they sailed to Haifa in what was by then Israel (see panel on right). They were divided into different age groups and sent to live on **kibbutzim**.

A wonderful surprise

As Bella was getting on a truck to go to her kibbutz, an old woman came up. She asked if she was from Iasi, and if she knew Bella and Esther. The woman was her own mother, who had not recognized her. It was an amazing moment.

Israel was declared an independent country on 14 May 1948. This photo shows Israel's first Prime Minister, David Ben-Gurion, declaring the establishment of the State of Israel.

The State of Israel timeline

After the war, many Jews moved to Palestine and established the State of Israel.

1917 – Britain took over Palestine.

1936 to 1939 – Palestinian Arabs fought against British rule.

1947 – The **United Nations** planned to divide Palestine between the Jews and the Palestinians.

1948 – Jews established the State of Israel in most of what was Palestine.

Zionist   someone who believes that Jewish people should move to Palestine and create a Jewish state

Primo Levi

Primo Levi was born in Turin, Italy, in 1919 to a Jewish family. When he grew up, he became a chemist. In 1943, the **Nazis** invaded Italy. Primo became a **partisan** and fought against the Germans. He was caught in 1944 and sent to Auschwitz. Primo survived partly because he was a chemist. His skills were useful to the Germans. He worked in a factory near Auschwitz that made fake rubber.

Primo's luck

Just when the Germans emptied Auschwitz camp, Primo caught **scarlet fever**. This turned out to be lucky. They thought he was dead and left him behind. Soviet soldiers freed him when they liberated the camp in January 1945. Only 20 of the 650 Italian Jews sent to Auschwitz had survived.

The Italian writer Primo Levi, whose books remain popular today. They remind people in a very moving way about the terrible events of the Holocaust.

A guide talks to students at a memorial, built in memory of the Holocaust, in Miami Beach, Florida, in the United States.

Word Bank   scarlet fever   serious disease that causes fever and red marks on the skin

After the war, Primo returned to Turin and got married. He went back to his career as a chemist and began to write books about the **Holocaust**.

Guilt and shame

Primo published his last book in 1986, *The Drowned and the Saved*. He wrote about how he felt guilty. He had survived when most did not. It seemed to him that it was usually selfish or violent people who survived, or those who helped the Nazis. Some harmed others just to survive themselves. Primo felt he was living in place of those who had died. In 1987, after being depressed for a long time, Primo killed himself.

Many Jewish people who survived the war felt guilty that others had died. These Jewish children who survived Buchenwald **concentration camp** make the Jewish symbol of the **Star of David**, five years after the end of the **Holocaust**.

"In Germany they came first for the **Communists** and I didn't speak up because I wasn't a Communist.

Then they came for the Jews and I didn't speak up because I wasn't a Jew.

Then they came for the **trade unionists** and I didn't speak up because I wasn't a trade unionist.

Then they came for the Catholics and I didn't speak up because I was a Protestant.

Then they came for me – and by that time no one was left to speak up."

Pastor Martin Niemöller (a German churchman and a former U-boat commander). Niemöller supported the Nazis at first but then changed his mind and opposed them. He was sent to a concentration camp but survived the war.

Communists people who support Communism, which is a system of government where all the wealth is shared out equally

TIMELINE

1918   End of World War I.

1919   The **Nazi** Party (originally called the "German Workers' Party") is set up.

1921   Adolf Hitler becomes leader of the Nazi Party.

1929   The **Great Depression** begins in the United States.

1932   The Nazis are the most popular party in the German elections.

1933   Hitler is made leader of the Nazi Party.
Hitler becomes the ruler of Germany.
Concentration camps are set up.

1935   German Jews are stripped of their rights by new laws. Nazis ban Jews from serving in the army.

1936   Heinrich Himmler is appointed head of the German police.

1937   Hitler reveals war plans during Hossbach Conference.

1938   Germany invades Austria and part of Czechoslovakia.
The Nazis attack Jews in Germany and Austria during *Kristallnacht*.
Refugee children come to the United Kingdom on the *Kindertransports*.
Nazis order all Jews over the age of 15 to apply for identity cards.

1939   Germany invades the rest of Czechoslovakia and Poland.
World War II begins.
The Nazis set up **ghettos** for Jews.

1940   German armies conquer Denmark, Norway, Belgium, **the Netherlands**, Luxembourg, and France.
Hitler plans the invasion of the United Kingdom.

1941   **Death squads** are set up.
Germany invades Yugoslavia, Greece, and the **Soviet Union**.

1941	The first **death camps** are set up: Auschwitz-Birkenau and Chelmo.
1942	Nazis hold the Wannsee Conference, where they decide on the "Final Solution" policy to kill all the Jews in Europe in an organized way. More death camps are set up: Sobibor, Treblinka, Belzec, and Majdanek.
1943	The Warsaw ghetto uprising against the Nazis. Heinrich Himmler orders the closing of the ghettos. The Vilna ghetto uprising.

1944

January	Soviet troops start to advance into Poland.
June	Allied forces enter Rome, Italy.
	Allied troops land in Normandy, France (D Day).
July	Soviet forces free prisoners in Majdanek death camp.
August	The Allies free Paris; Soviet troops take Bucharest, Romania.
October	The Allies free Athens, Greece; Germans surrender at Aachen.
	The last use of the **gas chambers** at Auschwitz.
1945	Allied troops free the surviving prisoners in the camps. World War II ends.
1945-46	Some leading Nazis are put on trial at the Nuremberg Trials. Some are put to death or imprisoned.
1948	The State of Israel is set up.
1953	Yad Vashem, the **Holocaust** Martyrs' and Heroes' Remembrance Authority, is established.

FIND OUT MORE

Search tips

There are billions of pages on the Internet so it can be difficult to find exactly what you are looking for. These search skills will help you find useful websites more quickly:

- Use simple keywords instead of whole sentences.

- Use two to six keywords in a search, putting the most important words first.

- Be precise – only use names of people, places or things.

- If you want to find words that go together, put quote marks around them.

Books

Here are just a few of the many books about the Holocaust.

Anne Frank, Cath Senker (Hodder Wayland, 2001)
A straightforward biography of Anne Frank.

The Complete Maus, Art Spiegelman (Penguin Books, 2003)
The story of the Holocaust retold in comic-strip form.

I Am David, Anne Holm (Harcourt, 2004)
The story of a young boy's journey through Europe after escaping from the camp where he has lived all his life.

In my Hands: Memories of a Holocaust Rescuer, Irene Gut Opdyke and Jennifer Armstrong
(Anchor Books/Doubleday, 2001)
The author tells how she, a young Polish girl, hid and saved Jews during the Holocaust.

Introducing the Holocaust, Haim Bresheet, Stuart Hood and Litza Jansz (Icon Books, 2000)
An introduction to the topic in comic-strip form.

Number the Stars, Lois Lowry
(Sagebrush Education Resources, 1999)
The story of a ten-year-old who helps to shelter her Jewish friend from the Nazis.

The Secret Room, Cynthia Mercati (Perfection Learning, 2000)
A Dutch girl helps to care for a Jewish family hiding in her father's church during World War II.

Uncle Misha's Partisans, Yuri Suhl (Shapolsky Books, 1988)
The story of an orphaned Jewish boy who joins a group of partisans in the Ukraine.

When Hitler Stole Pink Rabbit, Judith Kerr (Collins, 2002)
The story of a brother and sister who are rushed away from Germany in 1933.

DVD/VHS

Yellow Star – The Persecution of the Jews in Europe 1933–45 (VHS, 1994)
A documentary which looks at the persecution of the Jews in Europe between 1933 and 1945.

Websites

Search tips

Most sites are aimed at adults. They can contain upsetting information and pictures. Beware! A few people believe that the Holocaust was not very important, or even that it did not happen at all. They have websites that say they are giving the facts. Make sure that you use well-known sites with correct information, such as the ones below.

http://motlc.wiesenthal.com/pages
The Multimedia Learning Centre of the Museum of Tolerance.

http://www.bbc.co.uk/history/war/wwtwo/holocaust_survivors_gallery.shtml
Child survivors of the Holocaust who went to the UK on the *Kindertransport*.

http://www.bbc.co.uk/history/war/wwtwo/index_special.shtml#holocaust
Links to several sites about the Holocaust.

http://www.wiesenthal.com/mot/children/list1.cfm
All about the children of the Holocaust.

www.ushmm.org
The United States Holocaust Memorial Museum site.

Disclaimer

All the Internet addresses (URLs) given in this book were valid at the time of going to press. However, due to the dynamic nature of the Internet, some addresses may have changed, or sites may have ceased to exist since publication. While the author, packager, and publishers regret any inconvenience this may cause readers, no responsibility for any such changes can be accepted by either the author, packager, or the publishers.

Where to search

Search engine

A search engine looks through the entire web and lists all sites that match the words in the search box. It can give thousands of links, but the best matches are at the top of the list, on the first page. Try **bbc.co.uk/search**

Search directory

A search directory is like a library of websites that have been sorted by a person instead of a computer. You can search by keyword or subject and browse through the different sites like you look through books on a library shelf. A good example is **yahooligans.com**

GLOSSARY

Allies countries such as the United Kingdom, France, and the United States that fought against Nazi Germany

annexe building added on to another building to give more space

Aryans people from Germany and Scandinavia whom the Nazis thought were superior to everyone else

bribed gave something, such as money or favours, to someone in order to get them to behave in a certain way

civilian person who is not in the army

command post underground shelter for fighters in the ghetto

Communists people who support Communism, which is a system of government where all the wealth is shared out equally

concentration camp prison where the Nazis sent their enemies to teach them to be Nazis. Many thousands died in them.

convent place where nuns live and work

customs officers workers who check people's bags when they arrive in a different country. They make sure people have not brought in illegal goods.

death camp camp where Nazis sent Jews and others to be killed

death squads groups of Nazis whose job it was to shoot Jews

deport force someone to move to another country

dictator ruler who has complete power over a country

excrement solid waste from humans

gas chambers rooms used by the Nazis to gas people to death

ghetto part of a town, with a wall around it, where Jewish people had to live

Great Depression time from 1929 to 1939 when the United States and the European economies were doing very badly. Many people were poor and without jobs.

hack cut with rough, heavy blows

Holocaust the killing of millions of Jews and others by the Nazis

ID papers Nazi identity papers that included the person's name and showed if he or she was Aryan, Jewish, or Roma

Jewish Councils groups of Jewish people chosen to run a ghetto

kibbutz (plural **kibbutzim**) community set up by some Jewish people who settled in Palestine

labour camp prison where Jews and others were sent to work for the Germans

monastery place where monks live and work

Nazis people in the political party that ran Germany from 1933 to 1945

Netherlands, the country in Western Europe, also called Holland

orphanage home for children with no parents to care for them

Palestine country that was divided when Israel was formed in 1948

partisans people who formed armed groups to fight the Nazis

protests occasions when people show that they disagree with, or do not approve of, something

rations small amounts of food and fuel given to people so that they can survive

rebellion when a group of people join together to fight against the people who are in power

refugees people who are forced to leave their country

resettled moved to another place to live

resist fight back and refuse to do as you are told

Roma (gypsies) people who travel around to live and work

scarlet fever serious disease that causes fever and rcd marks on the skin

smuggle move goods or people secretly

Soviet Union country that once spread across northern Asia into Eastern Europe and included what is now Russia. Also known as the USSR.

SS special police force, set up in 1925, as Hitler's personal guards. The SS later ran the death camps.

Star of David symbol of Jewish identity

synagogues Jewish places of worship

trade unions workers' organizations that try to make things better for people at work

tuberculosis serious lung disease

underground movement group of people who secretly got together to fight the Nazis

United Nations organization made up of many countries that tries to solve world problems in a peaceful way

Zionist someone who believes that Jewish people should move to Palestine and create a Jewish state

INDEX

Titles in the *On the Front Line* series include:

Hardback   1 844 43690 X

Hardback   1 844 43689 6

Hardback   1 844 43692 6

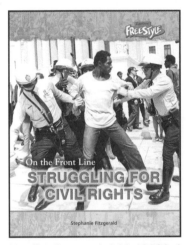

Hardback   1 844 43693 4

Hardback   1 844 43694 2

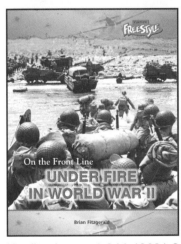

Hardback   1 844 43691 8

Find out about the other titles in this series on our website www.raintreepublishers.co.uk